Training Night

Sheila M. Blackburn

The fourth book in Set A of
Sam's Football Stories

Dedication

For my Mum.
With thanks to Tom for all the support and understanding.

Acknowledgements

With thanks to *The Boots Company* and *Delmar Press in Nantwich*, for their support of this project.

Published by Brilliant Publications
Unit 10, Sparrow Hall Farm
Edlesborough
Dunstable
Bedfordshire
LU6 2ES, UK

General information enquiries:
Tel: 01525 222292
Website: www.brilliantpublications.co.uk

The name Brilliant Publications and the logo are registered trademarks.

Written by Sheila M. Blackburn
Illustrated by Tony O'Donnell of Graham Cameron Illustration
© Sheila M. Blackburn 2002

Printed ISBN: 9781903853252
e-pdf ISBN: 9780857476173

ISBN 9781903853191 Set A - 6 titles: Football Crazy, Team Talk, Will Monday Ever Come?, Training Night, If Only Dad Could See Us! and a Place on the Team.
ISBN 9781903853030 Set B - 6 titles: The First Match, Trouble for Foz, What about the Girls?, What's Worrying Eddie?, Nowhere to Train and Are We the Champions?

First Published 2002. Reprinted 2006, 2009, 2015.
10 9 8 7 6 5 4

The right of Sheila Blackburn to be identified as the author of this work has been asserted by herself in accordance with the Copyright, Designs and Patents Act 1988.

At last it was Monday again.

"Training tonight," Sam said to himself.
He put another cross on his calendar.

Sam had a big breakfast.

"You're eating well, Sam," said Mum.

"I need the strength for training tonight," said Sam.

Mum smiled.
"I haven't forgotten," she said.
"Your kit will be ready when you come home from school."

"Great! Thanks, Mum," said Sam.
He put his coat on.

"Do try to be good at school today," said Mum.
"Try to think about your work and
not football all the time."

"OK, Mum," said Sam.
He set off happily to call for Danny.

Mondays can be very long days.
They are even longer if you have to wait for football training.

Sam did try hard – all day.

Even Miss Hill was pleased.
At the end of the day, she said,
"I hope the training goes well tonight, boys."

"Thanks, Miss," said Sam.

He and Danny ran all the way home.

"Have your tea now," said Mum.
"Then you won't feel too full at training."

Sam didn't want to stop and eat.

Mum had made his favourite: her own pizza with potato letters. She had done chocolate milkshake and there was ice-cream to follow.

"Wow!" said Sam. He sat down at the table.

"A special meal for a special night," said Mum.
"Eat up before it gets cold."

After tea, Sam had a rest.
He tried to watch TV, but his mind wasn't on it.

He went up to his room to sort out his kit.
Mum had put it on the bed for him.
She was really keen!

Sam put his United top, shorts and socks
into his United bag.

He took his school clothes off and put on his
jeans, top and trainers.

Downstairs, he got his boots and a plastic bag in case
they got muddy.

"I'm ready!"

"You're early," said Mum.

"I know," said Sam. "But I'm going now."

"Have a good time, then," said Mum.
"See you later."

Sam called for Danny.
He was just coming out of the door.

They half ran, half jogged to the Scout Hut.
It was further than the wasteland, but
it didn't take too long.

Eddie's old bike was up against the wall.

He was just unlocking the door when they arrived.
Rob and Foz were waiting at the corner.

"Hello, lads!" said Eddie.
"Come on in."

Eddie pushed his old bike inside.
The boys followed.

Eddie showed them to a little room.

"You can get changed in here," he said.

"Hang your coats up. Leave things tidy, please."

The room was soon full of shouts and calls.

Eddie blew a whistle.

Sam's Football Stories

"OK. Calm down a bit," he said.
"Now, when you're ready, come into the big room.
No boots indoors, please."

Eddie went out again.

Sam and Danny were ready first.

They carried their boots
and padded into the big room in their socks.

"Sit anywhere," said Eddie.

Soon, all the lads had come into the room.

Sam looked around.

He knew most of them.
They were from his class, or Mrs Day's class.

"Right, lads," Eddie was saying.
"Welcome to the first training session.
Just a few things to do before we start."

He wrote all their names in a book.
Then he told them about paying for each session.

"I've got a letter to give you
before you go home tonight," he said.
"It tells you about the number of sessions
and all my plans. That's later,
but right now – we'll do some training!
Follow me out onto the field.
You can put your boots on at the side of the hut."

There was a big rush for the door.

It was cold outside.

Sam's Football Stories

Sam was so excited he had a job to tie his laces.

Eddie was in his college tracksuit.
He had a big net full of footballs.
"When you're ready," he said,
"get a ball between three or four and do a bit of passing."

Sam and Danny got into a group with Rob and Foz.

Foz had a shirt that
come down to his
knees.
He was good at
passing.
He was good at
everything in
football.

When they had all
tied their boots,
Eddie said they had
to warm up.
"Like this," he said.

He began with on-the-spot jogs, bounces and star
jumps.

The boys did the same.

He waved his arms like a windmill.

The boys did it too.

With feet apart, he touched his toes.
Left, right. Left, right.

They all did it.

Next, they jogged round the field.
It was muddy in one corner.

Splish, splash. One lap.

Splish, splash. Two laps.

Mouse fell over in the mud.

Sam wanted to laugh, but he was too short of breath.

"Come on, lads. Faster!" shouted Eddie.

"He is fit, isn't he?" said Tim.

Sam and Danny were jogging together.
Even they had stopped talking.
Everyone was worn out after two laps.
Eddie looked at all the red faces.
"I think we'll stop the warm up now," he said.

"Let's try some skills.
I want to see what you can do".

They did some dribbling.
Some of the boys stood in a line.
The rest had to dribble in and out between them.
Then they changed over.

Eddie put them into two teams.

They did the dribbling again, but now
it was a sort of race.
Sam and Danny were not on the same team.
Sam's team lost.

Danny made a face at Sam.
Sam looked away. He didn't care.

He was having such a good time – doing what real
footballers did.

After the dribbling, they tried some shooting.

Eddie was in goal.

The lads had to dribble in and shoot.

Eddie dived this way and that.
He was good at this too.
It was hard to get one past him.

They had three shots each.

Sam's Football Stories

Eddie saved most of them. Then he let a few in.
Foz scored two goals.

Tim fell over his laces.

David got mad because he didn't score.
He sat down and sulked at the back of the goal.

"He always does that at school," said Sam.

"He likes to win," said Danny.

Before the end of the session,
they played a short game.
It was eight a-side and Eddie was the referee.
The lads took turns to be in goal.

Foz was on Sam's team.
After a while, he ran down the wing.
He beat the keeper and scored.
He jumped and punched his fist in the air.
"YES!" he shouted.

David was goalie at the time and he was cross.
"Offside!" he yelled.

Eddie was on the spot.
"Not offside," he said.

"You defenders need to do some tackling.
Eddie looked at his watch.
Time to stop already.
He blew his whistle for the end of game.

"Not fair!" said David.

He kicked the grass hard.

Eddie looked at David and shook his head. "Thanks, lads," he said.

"Can't we go on a bit longer?" Sam asked.

"Sorry, no. We have to be out before the Scouts get here."

They all walked back over to the hut.

"Boots off here, please," said Eddie.
"Bang them on the edge of the path to get the mud off."

The air was filled with a lot of banging and thumping sounds.

It felt cold now that they had stopped running.
"Hurry up inside to get changed," said Eddie.

Sam padded back inside in his socks.

He stuffed his muddy boots into the plastic bag.
His muddy United kit went into the United bag
in a big heap.

"Ready, Danny?"

At the door, Eddie gave them a letter each.
"Give this to your mum or dad."

"Thanks, Eddie. Great!
See you next week."

Training Night

"Hope so, lads. Take care, now.
I enjoyed it too. I really did.
Mind how you go now."

Outside, it was getting dark.
Some grown-ups were waiting.
Sam saw his mum and waved.
He gave her the letter.

"Walk with us, Danny," she said.
"I told your mum I'd see you home."

Sam looked up at her and grinned.

"Well?" she said.
"You look tired."

"Worn out," said Danny. "And I'm hungry too."

"Well?" she said again.

She was smiling at Sam.
He knew that smile.

"It was brilliant," he said. "Just ace!
Can't wait till next week."

We hope that you enjoyed this book. To find out what happens next, look for the next book in the series.

Set A

> Football Crazy
> Team Talk
> Will Monday Ever Come?
> Training Night
> If Only Dad Could See Us!
> A Place on the Team

Set B

> The First Match
> Trouble for Foz
> What about the Girls?
> What's Worrying Eddie?
> Nowhere to Train
> Are We the Champions?

Sam's Football Stories

www.ingramcontent.com/pod-product-compliance
Lightning Source LLC
Chambersburg PA
CBHW060553030426
42337CB00019B/3536